Where the Spirit
of the
Lord Is

By: Dr. J. T. Flowers

*Now the Lord is the Spirit; and where
the Spirit of the Lord is, there is liberty.*
-II Corinthians 3:17 (NKJV)

Llumina
Christian
Books

Where the Spirit of the Lord Is
ISBN 16255039-2-X
Copyright 2010 by Jacqueline T. Flowers

Published by Jacqueline T. Flowers
P.O. Box 671522
Houston, Texas 77267-1522

ISBN: 978-1-62550-392-3

Printed in the United States of America by Llumina Christian Books

Table of Contents

Chapter One

How God Leads Us into Liberty

The foundational scripture of this book comes from the following scriptural reference:

II Corinthians 3:17-18
Now the Lord is the Spirit; and where the Spirit of the Lord is, there is liberty. But we all, with unveiled face, beholding as in a mirror the glory of the Lord, are being transformed into the same image from glory to glory, just as by the Spirit of the Lord.

The emphasis of this book is two-fold: (1) to ensure that none of us are ignorant of satan's devices; his strategy; his methods; wiles (methods of entrapment; schemes of deception); and (2) to provoke growth so that we are ever maturing in the knowledge of Christ and exemplifying that knowledge in our day to day activities.

We should always leave a teaching with a greater level of insight than before. We should leave every teaching with an aspiration to develop the more. We should leave every teaching with a mind to excel; a mind to demonstrate a greater level of loyalty; a greater level of commitment to Christ; a deeper passion to show others the way to Christ.

This teaching requires that we understand the authority of God and submit ourselves there unto. Authority is simply God's plan by which to protect us and keep us in step with His will for our lives.

Man can only enjoy freedom, the ultimate liberty, through submission to the authority of God. Submission to God is obedience to the Word of God. The Greek word for obedience is "hupakoe," and it refers to the new life in Christ, which requires total submission to the Word of God; to hear with a readiness, a will to surrender all for the purpose of following the instructions of God; a readiness to rearrange one's entire life to accommodate the Truth.

There are things about Christ we will know only as we obey Him. Obedience will lead us into greater insight into the person of Christ, and greater revelation of the endless possibilities we enjoy just because of our union with Christ.

Independent of God and obedience to His instructions, there is no liberty, no freedom, and no deliverance. Anytime we place a tradition, a doctrine, a person, or an activity above the Word of God, we are enslaved thereby and cannot taste the reality of true liberty.

It is absolutely essential that we each have a firm grasp on the liberty we enjoy in Christ. If we are void of a sound understanding of this liberty, we will be a candidate for deception, never enjoying the fullness of our rights in Christ. The devil's aim is to lure us down a path of deception through temptations that remove us from under the umbrella of God's hand of protection.

The devil seeks to enslave so that man never comes into the knowledge of Truth. He does not care what or whom he uses; he is focused and perfected in evil.

God does not want us in bondage to a tradition; bondage to a denomination; bondage to a thought pattern; bondage to a habit; bondage to a relationship; bondage to an activity; bondage to an organization. God does not want to bind us. He sent His Son so that you and I would experience the ultimate freedom.

Hebrews 1:1-14

God, who at sundry times and in divers manners spake in time past unto the fathers by the prophets, Hath in these last days spoken unto us by His Son, whom He hath appointed heir of all things, by whom also He made the worlds; Who being the brightness of His glory, and the express image of His person, and upholding all things by the word of His power, when He had by Himself purged our sins, sat down on the right hand of the Majesty on high: Being made so much better than the angels, as He hath by inheritance obtained a more excellent name than they. For unto which of the angels said He at any time, Thou art My Son, this day have I begotten thee? And again, I will be to Him a Father, and He shall be to me a Son? And again, when He bringeth in the firstbegotten into the world, He saith, And let all the angels of God worship Him. And of the angels He saith, Who maketh His angels spirits, and His

3

> *ministers a flame of fire. But unto the Son He saith, Thy throne, O God, is for ever and ever: a sceptre of righteousness is the sceptre of Thy kingdom. Thou hast loved righteousness, and hated iniquity; therefore God, even thy God, hath anointed Thee with the oil of gladness above thy fellows. And, Thou, Lord, in the beginning hast laid the foundation of the earth; and the heavens are the works of Thine hands: They shall perish; but Thou remainest; and they all shall wax old as doth a garment; And as a vesture shalt Thou fold them up, and they shall be changed: but Thou art the same, and Thy years shall not fail. But to which of the angels said He at any time, Sit on My right hand, until I make thine enemies thy footstool? Are they not all ministering spirits, sent forth to minister for them who shall be heirs of salvation?*

Therefore intense discipline is required to stand fast; to submit to God; to heed the instructions of God; to remain in position with God.

None of us can remain in position with God if we are not willing to submit to the authority of God. We cannot move forward if we refuse to stay in position with God. The ability to truly put into practical application principles essential to successful Christian living requires that God's Word be the governing authority in our lives.

The purpose of this is book is to bring us into full awareness of the liberty extended to everyone who accepts

Jesus Christ as Savior and Lord. The ministry of Jesus Christ is a ministry of liberation, not manipulation, abuse, seduction, or control. It is the ministry of freedom.

The objective of this book is to challenge us to be a liberated church; to truly enjoy Christ. God wants to change the face of the local church. He wants an atmosphere of liberation in His house; an atmosphere of jubilation.

It's time to rejoice, and again I say rejoice! Joy produces power. Joy releases power. Joy empowers us to withstand trouble. The word "enjoy" means to have and experience life with joy; to be glad; to receive pleasure from; to have the use and benefit of; to rest in the position of advantage.

Joy empowers us to be perfected in the character of God. We demonstrate our gratitude by rejoicing, that is by thanking and praising God for the position we hold in Christ, and all the benefits belonging to us by virtue of this covenant relationship. God wants us to demonstrate our appreciation for Him and all He has done for us in our attitude, in our speech, in our conduct, and in a lifestyle of service to suffering humanity.

We are benefactors of grace. God owes us nothing, and yet, we owe Him everything.

God wants the kind of atmosphere in our lives and in His local church that attracts the lost to the Lord Jesus Christ; the kind of atmosphere that has no allowance for sin and no platform to accommodate any degree of darkness.

God wants an aroma about us that stimulates others to have a passion for Him. God wants an atmosphere that is so charged with the life of God, wherein we are not even tempted to go back into what God has so graciously brought us out of. This atmosphere of freedom should not just be visible around the saints, but it should be a lifestyle.

The goal of this book is to attract the lost, the sinners, the backslider, the brokenhearted, the oppressed, and the captives through our liberation. God wants His Church to fully express the power of liberation so that sinners are attracted to the Body of Christ. He wants us to stand fast and fully express our freedom in Christ as we represent Christ.

We are the offspring of God; a product of God positioned in time for the purpose of representing God in this earth. The word "represent" means to re-present; present again; to present a likeness or image of; to flaunt a picture of God so as to create a desire in the heart of another; to be a sign or symbol for; to stand as an authorized agent for; to speak and behave as an ambassador for God.

God wants us to represent Him by being the Word made flesh.

What Is Liberty in Christ?

Galatians 5:1
Stand fast therefore in the liberty wherewith Christ hath made us free, and be not entangled again with the yoke of bondage.

Lamentation 1:9b
Jerusalem forgot her destiny; her fall was awesome.

Christ brings a liberty that removes all darkness, all death, all defeat, and all ignorance. We must never forget the power of what God has done for us through His Son. We have been called unto liberty. God created man to be free, and as long as man remains obedient to God, he can experience nothing less than freedom; nothing less than liberty.

The word liberty comes from the Greek word "eleutheria", and it means (1) filled with the blessing of grace; (2) positioned to enjoy the benefits of God's love; (3) freedom; (4) generosity (we are now generous because we are recipients of the generosity of God); (5) boldness; (6) the flaunting of grace; (7) no longer enslaved by the

7

bondage of corruption; (8) independence from the world and the god of this world system, to dependence upon God; (9) deliverance of the sinner from the power of sin, not the presence of sin.

The liberty that Christ extends to us is a liberty that brings joy; a liberty that brings enthusiasm; a liberty that lifts up the hung down head; a liberty that puts a skip in our steps; a liberty that removes all shackles; a liberty that puts a clap in our hands; a liberty that puts a song upon our lips; a liberty that puts a dance in our feet; a liberty that brings a smile to the countenance; a liberty that brings a message of hope; a liberty that brings a radiance to the countenance so powerful that it attracts sinners; a liberty that brings a peace, that calmness of spirit and rest of mind; a liberty that restores wholeness to a broken and shattered life; a liberty that brings the expectation for a brighter tomorrow; a liberty that gives birth to an expectation of good and not evil; a liberty that reinforces a Godly perspective in the midst of trouble; a liberty that brings empowerment to resist sin and exercise self-government; a liberty that removes far from us a spirit of heaviness; a liberty that simply says, "I am free!"

This liberty says that we are free from the dominion of satan; free from the torment of sin; free from all guilt, shame, and condemnation; free to live; free to soar; free from the opinions of man.

Just free! Free to be whole. Free to be complete. Free to be successful. Free to be who God created us to be. Free to be happy. Free to arise. Free to move forward and never look back. Free in our minds. Free! Free to enjoy the abundant life.

Heaviness does not come from God.

Isaiah 61:3

To appoint unto them that mourn in Zion, to give them beauty for ashes, the oil of joy for mourning, the garment of praise for the spirit of heaviness; that they might be called trees of righteousness, the planting of the Lord, that He might be glorified.

Fear of dread or evil does not come from God. (**Jeremiah 29:11**) Bondage and shame does not come from God.

Jesus does not leave us like He found us. Life is always better once we are in union with Christ. When we understand the power of our liberty, there will be a passion to share this new life with others as Ambassadors for Christ.

Luke 4:18-21

The Spirit of the Lord is upon Me, because He hath anointed Me to preach the gospel to the poor; He hath sent Me to heal the broken-hearted, to preach deliverance to the captives, and recovering of sight to the blind, to set at liberty them that are bruised, to preach the acceptable year of the Lord. And He closed the book and He gave it again to the minister and sat down. And the eyes of all them that were in the synagogue were fastened on Him. And He began to say unto them, This day is this scripture fulfilled in your ears. (**Isaiah 61:1**)

What an awesome privilege to be a Christian, a follower of Christ! What an awesome privilege to have life and that more abundantly! How awesome it is to be free from the dominion of sin? What an awesome opportunity to be kin to God! What an honor to be the offspring of God!

Liberation does not mean anything goes. Liberation does not mean we are free to sin. Liberation means we are free from the sting of death which is sin. Christ has called us to a liberty that empowers us to submit to the restrictions of the covenant we have with Christ. While we are free in Christ, we are not free to disobey Christ.

Matthew 7:13-14 (KJVB)

Enter ye in at the strait gate: for wide is the gate, and broad is the way, that leadeth to destruction, and many there be which go in thereat: Because strait is the gate, and narrow is the way, which leadeth unto life, and few there be that find it.

Matthew 7:13-14 (Message Bible)

Don't look for shortcuts to God. The market is flooded with surefire, easy-going formulas for a successful life that can be practiced in your spare time. Don't fall for that stuff, even though crowds of people do. The way to life—to God—is vigorous and requires total attention.

We must endeavor to truly apprehend what Christ has accomplished so much so that we can't stop rejoicing. We can't stop thanking God. We can't stop shouting. We can't stop dancing. When we have a revelation concerning this liberty in Christ, we can never walk in God's house or in

His presence with a sad face or a heavy heart. Jesus brought liberation. Are others able to see that liberation? Are others able to see that freedom?

The thing that fuels life is the liberty that generates a passion for God's Will. When we refuse to seek God's Will, we are only stealing from ourselves. Jesus said, *I am come that they might have life, and life more abundantly.* (**John 10:10**)

When the Spirit of the Lord is present within us, there is life. There is liberty. There is fulfillment. There is wholeness. Where the Spirit of the Lord is there is freedom. When the Spirit of the Lord is present, we are enveloped in an aura of power, an aura of passion. Life is not miserable. Life is exciting. We all face challenges, but liberty empowers us to see every challenge through the unfailing ability of God.

When the Spirit of the Lord is present, there is joy. When the Spirit of the Lord is present, there is commitment. When the Spirit of the Lord is present, there is loyalty. When the Spirit of the Lord is present there is radiance. There is an aroma that dwells within that permeates through to our countenance and our demeanor. Everything about us says we are united to the Father through the Son. **There is nothing sad about us.** We should be so enthused over what God has done and what God is doing!

God does not want to destroy, He wants to save. God does not want to enslave us. His Will is to free us, and yet our freedom is proportional to the level of truth we embrace and allow to govern our lives. Jesus said, *and ye shall know the Truth and the Truth shall make you free.* (**John 8:32**)

When the character of the person of the Holy Spirit dwells in man, there is an implosion (burst of power that promotes enthusiastic purity, service, praise and worship). There should be a bursting inward, a sudden rush of power that causes us to never accept defeat; never accept depression; never accept discouragement. Daily our lives should be filled with energy, an excitement that transcends all of the ills of life. We are here on this planet for more than working an eight hour job. God did not put us here to wander aimlessly through time never enjoying the good life He prearranged for us to live.

Ephesians 2:10
For we are God's workmanship, created in Christ Jesus to do good works, which God prepared in advance for us to do.

Chapter Three

Understanding the Power of Liberty

We are in this world, but not of the world. Physically and geographically, we are on planet earth, but we are not a product of planet earth.

He removes the veil (an inability to see and change; blindness) so that born again man can see and be transfigured into the very image that he sees, the image of Christ. (**II Corinthians 3:17**)

God wants Christ formed in us. He wants the life of Christ to be visible due to internal conformity to the character of Christ, so that external righteous behavior is automatic; simply a result of us being molded and shaped by the Word of God. **We are called to be Word shaped.** The evidence that Christ is formed in us is holiness; a lifestyle of power enabling us to resist the pull, the power, and the persuasion of sin.

Galatians 4:19
My little children, of whom I travail in birth again until Christ be formed in you...

How do we see Christ? We see Christ in the mirror, that being the Word of God. We are transfigured when we choose to be shaped and molded by the Word of God.

13

When we consider all that Christ has done for us and in us, life should be a continual celebration. We should be so passionate about our relationship with Christ until nothing and nobody can steal our enthusiasm for God and towards God.

Enthusiasm comes from two Greek Words, "en", which means "in," and "Theos", which means God; thus we have "in God"; inspired by God; a glory not upon like Moses, but a glory within. Why within? The glory of God must be within for the purpose of releasing without (let God out; let God be seen).

We have this treasure in earthen vessels. The glory of God, the Spirit of God; the anointing that destroys every yoke of bondage; every addictive yoke; every oppressive yoke.

God's Spirit within us brings joy, not sorrow; freedom rather than struggle. He is our Enabler; the One who enables us keep God's commandments.

II Corinthians 4:1-7

Therefore seeing we have this ministry, as we have received mercy, we faint not; But have renounced the hidden things of dishonesty, not walking in craftiness, nor handling the Word of God deceitfully; but by manifestation of the truth commending ourselves to every man's conscience in the sight of God. But if our gospel be hid, it is hid to them that are lost: In whom the god of this world hath blinded the minds of them which believe not, lest the light of the glorious gospel of Christ,

14

Who is the image of God, should shine unto them. For we preach not ourselves, but Christ Jesus the Lord; and ourselves your servants for Jesus' sake. For God, who commanded the light to shine out of darkness, hath shined in our hearts, to give the light of the knowledge of the glory of God in the face of Jesus Christ. But we have this treasure in earthen vessels, that the excellency of the power may be of God, and not of us.

The word "veil" in the Greek is "katapetasma" and it metaphorically means "the flesh of Christ" (**Hebrews 10:20**) in that His body was broken for us, which He gave up to be crucified. This provided the spiritual access of believers to the Father; the new and living way. Through the blood and the body of Christ, we are qualified to enter into the presence of God and enjoy this new life.

The veil that Moses put upon his face illustrated not just the affect of him being in the presence of God, but also the fading of the Old Covenant and the veil upon the minds of the people. The veil upon their minds kept them from understanding the New Covenant and the forth coming redemptive work of Christ.

The Old Testament was fading in glory. The New Testament was the fulfillment of the Old, which established a better Covenant built upon better promises; a glory within. Christ in the hope of glory!

The word "veil" in the Greek is "kalumma" and it means to blind; a covering as used of the veil which Moses put over His face when descending Mount Sinai, thus preventing

Israel from beholding the glory. (**II Corinthians 3:13-17**)
This speaks metaphorically of the spiritually darkened life
without Christ and the spiritually darkened vision suffered
by Israel, until the conversion of the nation to their Messiah
takes place.

God's Word is Truth and God cannot lie. God does not
half save us or half deliver us.

John 8:31
*Jesus says, If you abide in My Word, you are
My disciples indeed. And you shall know the
truth, and the Truth shall make you free.*

If we say we are born of God's Spirit; if we say we are
abiding in His Word, **freedom should be the by product.** If
we are not free; if we are still bound; if darkness is present,
we are not abiding in the Truth and God is not present.

If we are free, we ought to behave like free men. If we
are truly liberated, we should behave like liberated people.
Regardless of our basic personality, liberty in Christ will be
seen. Freedom cannot be concealed.

We must refuse to allow the devil to steal our enthusiasm.
We must not let the devil steal our passion for Christ.
He comes to steal, kill, and destroy. We must stand fast
(**Galatians 5:1**) because his aim is to trip us up with the
cares of this life, the deceitfulness of riches and the lust of
other things.

Deuteronomy 28:45-47
*Moreover all these curses shall come upon
thee, and shall pursue thee, and overtake*

thee, till thou be destroyed; because thou hearkenest not unto the voice of the Lord Thy God, to keep His commandments and His statutes which He commanded thee: and they shall be upon thee for a sign and for a wonder, and upon thy seed forever. Because thou servest not the Lord Thy God with joyfulness ,and with gladness of heart, for the abundance of all things;

God wants us to celebrate our new life in Christ. He wants a continual celebration. The world has yet to truly see the true church, because we have allowed so many distractions to smother our enthusiasm. This is not an emotional teaching. God's objective is not to stir us emotionally, but rather to stir up the Body of Christ spiritually so that we are the effective witnesses He called us to be.

God wants us to flaunt this liberty that has been bestowed upon us. The internal liberty we enjoy should be seen on the outside. He has given the name, Time of Celebration, to our local church for purpose. Consistent with His unchanging nature, God always reveals the purpose of a person, or a thing in the name of that person or thing.

We celebrate events such as the birth of a new baby, weddings, home purchases, graduations, and anniversaries; but more so, we are here to bring about a celebration in the earth realm. This is a celebration of liberation!

Liberation in Christ in its simplest form is enjoying Christ; flaunting Christ; sharing Christ through a liberated lifestyle. When God says we are free indeed, indeed we are free. We must walk in this freedom; walk in this liberty; live it out. We should look like the victorious people we are. The devil loves to play games with those who have not learned how to control their emotions and their thoughts.

II Corinthians 10:4-5

(For the weapons of our warfare are not carnal, but mighty through God to the pulling down of strong holds;) Casting down imaginations, and every high thing that exalteth itself against the knowledge of God, and bringing into captivity every thought to the obedience of Christ;

Do we enjoy what Christ has done? Do we appreciate what Christ has done? There should be joy in Christ.

Chapter Four

Why Do We as Christians Have Liberty?

*T*oo often we love the theatrics and the spectacular that we see in churches. We define church by the level of entertainment and the falling out. We judge a move of God by the level of emotions rather than the simplicity of truth being deposited into the hearts of men. We don't look for the reality of a passionate liberty; a passionate fervor. The passion of Christ should be our passion.

Jesus was a man of great passion. When He spoke of His Father, He spoke with passion. When He explained a parable to His disciples, He did so with passion. When He fed the five thousand, He did so demonstrating His passion for lost humanity. When He rebuked the Scribes, Pharisees, and Sadducees, He rebuked them with a deep passion for righteousness, and a passionate hatred towards hypocrisy and all sin. He cast out devils with authority and passion.

John 2:17
And his disciples remembered that it was written, The zeal of thine house hath eaten me up.

We should be passionate about what God is passionate about. God works mightily in the lives of those whose hearts are truly committed to Him and passionate about His affairs.

God does not want reluctant, half-hearted, ritualistic compliance. God wants enthusiastic obedience, and passionate praise & worship that stems from a vibrant love relationship with Him. When problems, distractions, and other things steal our devotion, our time, and our commitment, those other things become our god, thereby rendering us powerless to the kingdom of God.

The evidence of our union with Christ is His character and nature being present in our lives. God brings liberty because He wants us free from the cares of this life. When truth is accepted, the level of liberation revealed in our lives is proportional to that level of Truth we have accepted.

When we lack liberty, we are passion deficient. This simply says we have not totally accepted God's Word as Truth. We have not engaged and totally embraced the life that God has positioned us to live. When you and I are void of liberty and deficient of a passion that can only come from a life yielded to Christ, we are still holding on to the pleasures of sin somewhere in our lives. We have not yet become one with God.

Sin kills passion for holiness. Sin robs us of freedom. **Sin kills**. **Sin brings death**. Obedience brings blessings. Obedience relieves us of all fear and tension. Obedience brings peace. Obedience brings life.

Liberty in Christ says, "I am going all the way with Jesus. I am unstoppable and unbeatable. I will flaunt this liberty." To flaunt this liberty is a result of revelation knowledge.

Revelation knowledge that says, "I truly grasp the depth of what Christ accomplished for me when He hung on the cross on Calvary and got up out of the grave after three days and three nights."

What is that revelation? It is an honor to be chosen by God. It is an honor to be God indwelt. It is an honor that God would dare to allow the stench of us to be washed away with the blood of Jesus. It is an honor to be identified with God as His offspring. It is an honor to walk with the King of kings and Lord of Lords. It is an honor to know that God has withdrawn His wrath. It is an honor to know that God has wrapped us in His grace; His unfailing ability. It is an honor to know that God has made us a habitable place. It is an honor to know that we are already blessed coming in and blessed going out. **It is an honor!**

There should be a permanent smile fixed upon our faces when we consider what the Lord of Glory has done in us, is doing in us, and has done for us. Where is the life? Where is the passion? Where is the excitement? Where is the joy? Where is the God who indwells us? Have we forgotten this truth? How can we be stiff-necked and defiant when God could have wiped us off the face of the earth a long time ago?

Instead, He made a choice to die for us that we may live. Is it not an honor to know that we are the redeemed of the Lord? Is it not an honor to know that Jesus came that we might have life and that life more abundantly? Is it not an honor to be used by God to reconcile lost men to our Creator? Is it not an honor to know that God delivered us from our greatest problem, that being eternal damnation?

We can miss the greatest move of God because we lack the passion to see beyond our problems. Serving God is not a waste of time. Worshipping God is not a waste of time. Both have an eternal impact.

Jesus was filled with intense zeal for the will of God. The Greek word for "zeal" is "zelos," and it means intense enthusiasm, as in working for a cause; devotion; passion; to be excited.

I Samuel 17:29
….Is there not a cause?

John 2:17b
….The zeal of thine house hath eaten me up.

The life of Jesus was charged with passion to redeem us, so much so that Jesus said:

Hebrews 10:7
"Then said I, Lo, I come (in the volume of the Book it is written of Me,) to do Thy Will, O God.

To live a life engaged in liberty and joy, we must each understand the difference between passion and obligation.

When we get up and go to work, many of us see it as an obligation; just a job. We will thus behave and perform up to the level of just being hired to do a job. We complain and see the job through the eyes of a pay check only. When it's an obligation, we just go through the motions of doing what we have to do.

However, when passion is present, whatever the task, we work sacrificially and unconditionally as partners with the Lord. We are willing to rise early, stay up late, and work longer hours; be creative and innovative. Nobody motivates us. We do not need on-sight supervision. We remain committed and devoted to a cause. No one makes us show up when there is liberty, and thus passion.

No one has to beg us to get involved when we have tasted liberty. No one has to beg us to serve when passion is present. Being focused and faithful no matter the external circumstances is a product of passion. Calvary depicts God's passion for our dying human society. God does not want our service in ministry to Him to be done out of obligation, but rather out of love and passion. This is the same passionate love that prompted Him to die for us.

Attendance in Sunday Worship and Bible Study services should be a result of passion, not obligation. Giving financially to my local church should be a result of passion, not obligation. Being involved in my local church should be a result of passion, not obligation. Attending Biblical education classes should be a result of passion for the Word of God.

When we get off of work, we should be invigorated with a passion to get to God's house more than to our own home. No one can motivate us to be faithful to a God who poured out His blood for us. Passion is deeper than motivation, and liberty transcends obligation.

We are never too tired to get to God's House when we are passionate. When we are fueled by passion, one sermon is never enough. Often we start with passion, but soon, what we do becomes an obligation.

How many marriages start with passion, but soon become an obligation? How often does having a child start with a passion, but soon parenting the child becomes an obligation? How often does serving in ministry begin with a passion, and what was once a passion soon becomes just another obligation?

We lose the fervor, the zeal, the passion, and the excitement. When then begin to look externally for another marriage, another church, another job, or another ministry. We look externally instead of internally. We fail to look within.

The devil enslaves with a yoke of bondage. A yoke of bondage is a device to enslave; to restrict; to confine; to harness, to hold back, to torture, and torment; to manipulate, seduce, deceive, control, and destroy.

The Greek word for "bondage" is "douleia," and it refers to man's submission to some teaching, influence, or compulsion that enslaves and restrains him so that growth and development is not possible; the condition of being imprisoned so as to smother out any possible chance of escape; a deliberate mechanism by which to keep man from being fully reconciled to God.

Walking with Christ does not bring sadness; it brings joy. Being joined to Christ produces a life of internal rest, rather than worry, turmoil, or internal agitation. Walking with Christ does not bring bondage, it brings freedom. Walking with Christ is not a life of deprivation, but rather of life of abundance; a life of provision. (**Philippians 4:19**)

Walking with Christ produces a life of praise, adoration, and worship; not a spirit of heaviness.

Nehemiah 8:10b
....the joy of the Lord is your strength.

In the face of joy, there will always be the power to withstand the vicious assaults of the devil and his demons. There will always power to rise above the problems unique to just being in this world.

Christ adorns us with a yoke of freedom.

Matthew 11:25-28
At that time Jesus answered and said, I thank Thee, O Father, Lord of heaven and earth, because Thou hast hid these things from the wise and prudent, and hast revealed them unto babes. Even so, Father: for so it seemed good in Thy sight. All things are delivered unto Me of My Father: and no man knoweth the Son, but the Father; neither knoweth any man the Father, save the Son, and he to whomsoever the Son will reveal him. Come unto Me, all ye that labour and are heavy laden, and I will give you rest.

John 8:32-36
And ye shall know the truth, and the truth shall make you free. They answered him, "We be Abraham's seed, and were never in bondage to any man: how sayest thou, Ye shall be made free?" Jesus answered them," Verily, verily, I say unto you, Whosoever committeth sin is the servant of sin. And the servant abideth not in the house for ever: but the Son abideth ever. If the Son therefore shall make you free, ye shall be free indeed."

Christ brings the aroma of liberty to a life once held captive by the forces of evil. Christ brings a liberty that frees us from all dread of evil and all terror. (**I John 2:18-29; John 14:15-31**)

The traditions of men and self promoting doctrines only serve to deceive and enslave. (**Colossians 2:1-8; Matthew 15:1-9**)

Psalm 119:45

And I will walk at liberty: for I seek Thy precepts.

Chapter Five

How Liberty in Christ Affects the Lost

E vangelism becomes so much more effective when people can see in us what they need. It is so much more than an organized day of outreach.

So many are yet lost in sin, blind, alienated and shut off from the life of God; but you and I are here, saved, and empowered with the ability to see and know God; to experience Him and live free from the subtle entrapments of evil!

An atmosphere of liberation is an atmosphere of healing; an atmosphere of deliverance; an atmosphere of victory; an atmosphere of celebration; an atmosphere of love; **an atmosphere of power. Wherever there is liberty, there will be power.** God wants an atmosphere so charged with power that our marriages are getting stronger and more radiant; our unmarried adults are saturated with the teachings of Christ; our young people are on fire with revival; the elderly are skipping with joy and the onlookers have a passion to join us.

No one is drawn to bondage. Liberation has a drawing power. It expresses an attitude of victory; a disposition of triumph; an atmosphere of strength, an atmosphere of power; an atmosphere of deliverance from any yoke of bondage.

Why does God want us to celebrate our liberty in Christ? He wants to ignite hope in the hearts of the hopeless. He wants the sinners to see the power of authentic liberty so that they will be attracted to the Spirit of Liberty. There are no lasting results in artificial liberty, that being liberty which is fueled by drugs, alcohol, and sexual perversion. This only provides a temporary, artificial liberty.

God wants to use our liberty as a bright light, a drawing card to ignite a desire in the hearts of the unbelievers to seek Jesus Christ because He is the Way, the Truth, and the Life.

Who looks at us and wants to have what we have if they see defeat, worry, sickness, depression, discouragement, disappointment, deception, gossip, slander, a mean spirit and such like?

God called us the salt of the earth and the light of the world. God uses two powerful components to describe our level of potency and effectiveness – salt and light. Salt is a dominating seasoning that changes, preserves, and purifies. Light dispels all darkness. It is a dominating force.

Matthew 5:13-16

Ye are the salt of the earth; but if the salt have lost his savor, wherewith shall it be salted? It is thenceforth good for nothing, but to be cast out, and to be trodden under foot of men. Ye are the light of the world. A city that is set on a hill cannot be hid. Neither do men light a candle, and put it under a bushel, but on a candlestick; and

it giveth light unto all that are in the house.
Let your light so shine before men, that they
*may see your **good works**, and glorify your*
Father which is in heaven.

God wants the world to see our joy. He wants the world to experience our saltiness. He wants us to brighten up the atmosphere. He wants to stir us to appreciating the liberty we enjoy in Christ Jesus so others want that same liberty. God wants the world to see Holy Ghost fueled passion. This passion transcends feelings and emotions.

God does nothing independent of the Holy Spirit. Through the power of the Holy Spirit, He infuses us with a passion for God and a passion over what He has accomplished within us, and for us. True liberty in Christ gives birth to passion. Passion cannot be manufactured; it is a product of man's heart attitude towards God. Passion comes from within and is demonstrated without. **We must closely inspect what's happening within.**

The sinner should never wonder, "Where is the life? Why are they so depressed and defeated?" Sinners have more passion over sin than saints display over the blood of the Savior. If we do not remain passionate about our relationship with Christ, like a junky, we begin an endless, tormenting pursuit for a continuous fix to keep us going.

Christians should be full of fire; radical for Jesus; grasping and engaged in this life that Jesus purchased for us with His own blood. We should be proud to suffer death to the pleasures of sin for the purpose of sharing Christ with the lost.

Chapter Six

What Hinders Our Enjoyment of the Christian Life?

*L*et's consider these points so as to learn what hinders our enjoyment of the Christian life.

1. **Distractions** - We remove our eyes away from the great work God has accomplished in us and begin to lust after what is not ours to have; not now, not ever.

2. **The weight of problems** - The devil uses problems and adverse circumstances to suck the joy out of us. He uses trouble to steal our passion for Christ. He knows the power of liberty and passion. If the devil cannot persuade us to return to a life of sin, he just shoots problems our way until we are so preoccupied with the problem that we fail to realize we have the power to rise above the problem.

I Peter 4:12-14

Beloved, think it not strange concerning the fiery trial which is to try you, as though some strange thing happened unto you: but rejoice, in as much as ye are partakers of Christ's sufferings; that, when His glory shall be revealed, ye may be glad also with exceeding joy. If ye be reproached for the name of Christ, happy are ye; for the Spirit of Glory and of God resteth upon you: on their part He is evil spoken of, but on your part He is glorified.

I Corinthians 2:9-10
But as it written, Eye hath not seen, nor ear heard, neither have entered into the heart of man, the things which God hath prepared for them that love Him. But God hath revealed them unto us by His Spirit: for the Spirit searcheth all things, yea the deep things of God.

We never get involved in the great exploits which keep us ever expecting God for the next victory.

Daniel 11:32b
….but *the people that do know their God shall be strong, and do exploits.*

We can enjoy God and release a passion for the new life we enjoy in Christ. When passion meets potential, there will be great and might works. There will be an implosion! When passion, born out of liberty, meets potential, we refuse to exist. We must live. Passion triggers a no settling attitude; not when better and greater is possible.

The devil sends trials to steal our passion so that we never reach full potential, but here's the secret: **passion transcends trouble**. There is no problem, no test, and no assault of the devil that can stop us when we are passionate about God and what He has done to liberate us.

Potential is what God has given us the ability to do, that we have not come to realize that we can do. It is unrealized ability. Believe it or not, we can do better. We can achieve greater. We can go further.

Even in the midst of trouble, the internal presence of God Almighty; the internal regulation of the God's Spirit empowers us to soar far, far above the affects of trouble into His unlimited Grace, unlimited provision, and unlimited protection. God would not save us and not equip us with the empowerment to prevail over adversity.

Luke 17:21
....the kingdom of God is within us.

Success with God is not contingent upon what is happening around us, but rather what is happening inside of us. The smallness we experience comes from within us. There is nothing small or limiting about God. He reminds us that while we are finite creatures, He is the God of all flesh; there is nothing too hard for Him.

Our liberty in Christ transcends daily problems and adverse circumstances.

3. **We become lazy and refuse to serve in the local church.**

4. **We forget there is a press.** Walking in discipline and maintaining momentum is our responsibility.

5. **We are church goers**, not followers of Christ; religious, but not righteous.

6. **We lose our passion for the relationship because of sin**. Sin kills the desire for alone time with God. Thus our devotion (reading the Word of God; praise and worship; prayer; soul witnessing) becomes stale. God inspired us. He blew Himself into us for the purpose of establishing a powerful union with us. He put His divine influence within so as to stimulate us to passionately long for Him, worship Him, fellowship with Him, and share Him. All that is in God, He blew into us.

Ezekiel 11:19

And I will give them one heart, and I will put a new spirit within you; and I will take the stony heart out of their flesh, and will give them a heart of flesh: that they may walk in My statutes, and keep Mine ordinances, and do them: and they shall be My people, and I will be their God.

Israel is a type of the Body of Christ and today we are living in the reality of this passage. God has given us one heart, His heart. He has put a new spirit within us, that being the Spirit of the Lord. He has removed the nature of the devil and given us the nature of God. He has empowered us to walk in His statutes and keep His ordinances. We experience regeneration. Our spiritual DNA has changed.

In order to overcome those things that hinder our enjoyment of the Christian life, let us be mindful of these points in order to truly walk in the liberty that Christ has so freely given to us.

1. Remember to nurture and stir up an appetite for liberty. Stand fast because the devil will come to steal your liberty in Christ.

2. Refuse to allow people, places, and the past to define or distract us.

3. Remember that the level of success we experience and enjoy in this Christian life is always proportional to our level of obedience. Success is proportional to the truth we accept and govern our lives by.

4. Refuse to be deceived and allured by the pleasures of sin.

5. Remember that God gives victory to those who trust Him. If we consistently trust God over the course of our lifetime, we will see God usher us into plateaus of victory. We have been chosen by God, thereby equipped as citizens of heaven to overcome every obstacle; every hindrance.

6. Remember to meditate on our inheritance.

7. Refuse dissatisfaction. Dissatisfaction is a sign that we are not grateful and have lost the will to control the mind; program the mind; exercise the mind to accept truth as our reality.

8. Remember to offer praise continually and keep company with liberated people.

   He came that we might enjoy this new life.

   We should be enjoying life in Christ, no matter what season we are in.

Jeremiah 29:11
*For I know the thoughts that I think toward
you, saith the Lord, thoughts of peace, and
not of evil, to give you and expected end.*

We have the advantage. God's involvement in our lives
should never be taken for granted.

Chapter Seven

How and Why the Christian Should Enjoy the Christian Life

*L*et's consider these points so as to learn how to enjoy our liberty in Christ.

1. **Accept God's Word as Truth.** God did not create us to maneuver around in time in drudgery and despair.

Proverbs 27:19b (NKJVB)
...so a man's heart reveals the man.

What a man has accepted as truth, he will live, thus revealing the real man. We can only be as free as we are willing to yield to the transforming power of Truth. In other words, the level of victory seen in our lives, or the level of freedom seen in our lives, is proportional to the degree by which we accept God's Word as Truth and order our lives thereby. Man's finite mind cannot grasp God and the heavenly realities. This is why we are commanded to live by Faith. God is a heavenly reality and we can only know Him by accepting His Word as Truth.

There is a disparity between what we believe and what we say. **When we truly believe God's Word, it will be visible in our lives. Truth shapes our lives so that Truth is seen.**

Truth can only transform those who submit to it. When we are submitted to Truth, nobody has to beg us to be committed. Nobody has to beg us to worship. Nobody has to beg us to serve. **Nobody has to beg us to read the Bible. Nobody has to beg us to pray. Nobody has to beg us to attend Bible Study. Nobody has to beg us to come church. Nobody has to run a scheme on us to worship God with our tithes and offerings.**

We were placed in time to make a difference, and we should want to make a difference without the coercion of others.

We are not here for the big house, the automobile, the diamonds, furs, riches, land, and the celebrity status. Our joy is not dependent upon our career or our stuff. Our joy is spawned by a life of obedience to Christ; a life shaped by Truth.

We cannot fulfill God's purpose for the church without passion; without freedom; without liberty. Christians should be the most exciting, the most radical, the most enthusiastic, and the most passionate people on the face of the earth and this radical, enthusiastic life must be seen so that others can desire it.

People should look at us and long for the liberty we have; the passion we have; the joy we have. They should see that we are benefactors of the work of redemption; the work of Grace.

They should see that we see life in Christ as a gift; our natural life as well as our new spiritual life. All of us were created for a God ordained purpose.

John 8:32
And ye shall know the truth, and the truth shall make you free.

God has given us a liberty that causes us to rise above whatever we face in this life, knowing that what we face in time is temporary, but what we have within is eternal.

2. **Choose to be free.** Exercise the power of the will to reject all bondage. Will to embrace the liberty Christ extends.

John 8:36
If the Son therefore shall make you free, ye shall be free indeed.

It is possible to become comfortable and so accustomed to bondage that we resist freedom. We resist change. We resist liberty because we do not what to endure the hardships that come with change. We can be so comfortable with worry, fear, and dead end habits until we do not know how to function without them. **We become uncomfortable with freedom and free people.**

3. **Choose to reject small mindedness and simply make up your mind to rejoice!** Remove the limits off the mind. We can travel in life as far as we choose.

II Corinthians 6:11-13
(The Message Bible Translation)
Dear, dear Corinthians, I can't tell you how much I long for you to enter this wide-open, spacious life. We didn't fence you in. The smallness you feel comes from within you. Your lives aren't small, but you're living them

in a small way. I'm speaking as plainly as I can and with great affection (passion). Open up your lives. Live openly and expansively! (Live large)

Living large is not amassing materialistic wealth. Living large is not being dependent upon what one has externally. Living large means fulfilling God's will in life. It is abandoning our own thing so that we are truly free to do God's thing, whatever that thing may be. It is living life without limitations. It is investigating the possibilities; that is what could be if we remain connected to the True Vine and accept His Word as Truth.

Human talent and ability can take us so far. Traveling with God opens up endless possibilities that keep life exciting. It keeps passion alive.

We tend to confine God within the context of our own experiences. God is so much greater than our experiences. We must lift the limitations off of our own minds so that we can see how great God really is.

God is only limited in our lives because we have limited Him, just as the nation of Israel. (**Psalm 78**) He is an unlimited God, but we do not taste the unlimited possibilities because our minds are so small. We have limited God in our own minds, and thus we limit ourselves.

4. **Choose to never allow familiar spirits to oppress us.** We become familiar with the sermons, the anointing, the structure, and the order. We become familiar with God, and are no longer fiery for Him. Familiarity is a satanic method used to discourage passion and used to

discourage growth. As destructive as sinful habits are, we can prefer living with the familiar rather than being free to experience the unknown. **(Numbers 14) We take for granted our local church, our pastor, who God is, and what God has done. It is not until what we had is no longer accessible to us that we consider the value of what we had.**

5. **Choose to develop a Biblical perspective of God and abandon a human concept of God.** We cannot and we will not grow unless we have a healthy perspective of who God is and what God requires.

God is not waiting for us to mess up so that He can beat us down. He provides the strength and counsel necessary to show us where we are missing it so that we can come up to the standard.

A human concept is a generalized idea; not practical; not grounded; not based upon revelation from God. A human concept says, "If we do good God is with us, but if we mess up, God abandons us." The Truth that no matter what occurs, God is still with us and God is still for us, is a biblical perspective and not a concept. A biblical view of God and His grace says that He is still Jehovah-Shammah, no matter my weaknesses and frailties. **He still loves me.** The picture **God wants us to have of Him is one of Grace – unmerited favor – unearned and undeserved.** The example is seen in God's love and compassion towards Judas. Jesus knew that Judas was a betrayer when he selected him, and yet He chose him any way. You and I would not have made selection of Judas. He loved Judas as He loved all the disciples. Grace protects us and strengthens us. Jesus never exposed Judas. Judas exposed himself. Grace says, "I am for you and not against you." Grace says, "I know you are messing up and I am still here with you; pulling for you to overcome; pulling for you to get it right." God is more concerned about our success and victory than our failures. **He says He is for us. We will be miserable Christians unless we have a healthy perspective of God's love. All that we experience in God is a gift.**

I John 3:20-24

For if our heart condemn us, God is greater than our heart, and knoweth all things. Beloved, if our heart condemn us not, then have we confidence toward God. And whatsoever we ask, we receive of Him, because we keep His commandments, and do those things that are pleasing in His sight. And this is his commandment, That we should believe on the name of His Son Jesus Christ, and love one another, as He gave us commandment. And he that keepeth His commandments dwelleth in him, and He in him. And hereby we know that He abideth in us, by the Spirit which He hath given us.

II Corinthians 5:19-21

To wit, that God was in Christ, reconciling the world unto Himself, not imputing their trespasses unto them; and hath committed unto us the word of reconciliation. Now then we are ambassadors for Christ, as though God did beseech you by us: we pray you in Christ's stead, be ye reconciled to God. For He hath made Him to be sin for us, Who knew no sin; that we might be made the righteousness of God in Him.

This is not a license to sin. We do not need a license to sin. We have been sinning for a long time. A man does what he wants to do, regardless to what others say.

Galatians 4:4-9

But when the fulness of the time was come, God sent forth His Son, made of a woman, made under the law, to redeem them that were under the law, that we might receive the adoption of sons. And because ye are sons, God hath sent forth the Spirit of His Son into your hearts, crying, Abba, Father. Wherefore thou art no more a servant, but a son; and if a son, then an heir of God through Christ. Howbeit then, when ye knew not God, ye did service unto them which by nature are no gods. But now, after that ye have known God, or rather are known of God, how turn ye again to the weak and beggarly elements, whereunto ye desire again to be in bondage?

6. **Become skilled in hearing the Son by stilling yourself in the presence of God**. Busyness of mind and self-consumption are two of the greatest hindrances to growth and discerning the voice of God. We must be barrier breakers in our thinking. Barriers in the mind are real. They are fortresses; we allow nothing in and we do not get out. We must allow God's Word to enter as we destroy mental barriers. We must **saturate our minds with the Word of God daily. Rise above sensitivity to disappointments.** Resist and turn a deaf ear to every lie. There is nothing more powerful than hearing Jesus for yourself. Truth will expose every lie.

Lies oppose Truth. The devil is the originator, the father of lies. A lie is a deadly and contagious satanic message, communicated to others by a human agent so as to perpetuate its existence in the earth. The purpose of the lie is to contaminate the thought life of all that it comes in contact with, thereby influencing and stimulating ungodly behavior that triggers the release of deadly consequences. (**John 8:37-47**)

The devil's aim is to guarantee that a lie spreads. Therefore, it must be repeated in the earth by a human voice.

Matthew 17:1-5
And after six days Jesus taketh Peter, James, and John his brother, and bringeth them up into an high mountain apart, And was transfigured before them: and His face did shine as the sun, and His raiment was white as the light. And, behold, there appeared unto them Moses and Elias talking with Him. Then answered Peter, and said unto Jesus, Lord, it is good for us to be here: if Thou wilt, let us make here three tabernacles; one for Thee, and one for Moses, and one for Elias. While he yet spake, behold, a bright cloud overshadowed them: and behold a voice out of the cloud, which said, This is My beloved Son, in whom I am well pleased; hear ye Him.

7. **Know when to sleep and when to pray (Mark 14:32-42; Luke 9:28-35).**

8. **Refuse to be entangled again in the yoke of bondage. Don't go back.** Simply choose to be saturated with the oil of joy. We can enjoy a joy filled life by being perfected in the Fruit of the Spirit.

Galatians. 5:1
Stand fast therefore in the liberty wherewith Christ hath made us free, and be not entangled again with the yoke of bondage.

Isaiah 61:3
To appoint unto them that mourn in Zion, to give them beauty for ashes, the oil of joy for mourning, the garment of praise for the spirit of heaviness; that they might be called trees of righteousness, the planting of the Lord, that He might be glorified.

We have reiterated that where the Spirit of the Lord is there is Liberty. This is not merely a theological concept, but rather a profound reality in which we can place absolute confidence. It is not humanism; it is truth for meditation in all areas of life. It is a truth we can cling to in the midst of a hostile and perverse generation.

What we do reveals what we believe. If we are filled with fear and anxiety, we exemplify a frustrated, joyless life. We are proving our lack of confidence in God and the reality of every promise given to us as His offspring.

The joy of the Lord is our strength. It is the fruit of the Spirit. Joy is the nature and character of God, and those of us who possess His nature and character should be manifested in and through us in the form of joy.

John 16:23-24
And in that day ye shall ask Me nothing. Verily, verily, I say unto you, Whatsoever ye shall ask the Father in My name, He will give

it you. Hitherto have ye asked nothing in My name: ask, and ye shall receive, that your joy may be full.

John 15:11
These things have I spoken unto you, that My joy might remain in you, and that your joy might be full.

I John 1:4
And these things write we unto you, that your joy may be full.

When we consider that God saved us, how can we display anything less than a joy filled, liberated life? God has given us a divine birthright, a covenant relationship filled with benefits. What more could we ask? Why are we so joyless? Did God do His part or have we failed to accept what He has done and live in what He has done?

No circumstance of life should rob us of what God has done. The Spirit of the Lord gives us strength far beyond our own. Such power comes at God's discretion and for His purposes.

The victories we experience are not our own, despite our best effort. God provides them and makes them possible, and certainly they always benefit more than just us.

Problems can never rob us of our liberty in Christ. We all face problems. We all face temptations. At times, our strength may fail and our faith may wavier, but we have this hope: Christ our High Priest forever intercedes for us. He is victorious and will launch us into victory, if we will trust Him. He knows how to bring us out.

We can only be robbed of a benefit or a victory if we fail to accept God's promises as Truth and reject all that opposes that Truth.

Colossians 3:23-24
And whatsoever ye do, do it heartily (passionately) as to the Lord, and not unto men; knowing that of the Lord ye shall receive the reward of the inheritance for ye serve the Lord Christ.

The seed contains the fruit; we are born of the incorruptible seed of the Word of God. The invisible process of transformation soon shows up on the outside; and what joy, unspeakable and full of glory. As God enters our lives, we become like Him. Nothing stands between us and God. Our faces shine with the brightness of His face.

9. **Fellowship with others who are walking in the revelation of their liberty so as to guard your own liberty in Christ**. Build Godly relationships with people who are passionate about this new life in Christ. Discouragement and depression are contagious, so guard your liberty. Resist isolation and opposing doctrines. (**Proverbs 27:17**) Why is this essential? We can be saved but, still bound. (**Galatians 3:1-3**) Submission to the transforming power of God is the only way the grave clothes can be removed.

10. **Obey God's command to rejoice by memorizing and declaring all the scriptures you can on joy. Memorize and meditate on the power of joy.** Joy is not just a by-product of obedience to God. It is, in essence, obeying God. Joy is an essential part of our relationship with God.

We are commanded to rejoice in the Lord. If obedience is doing what God commands, then joy is not merely the spin off of obedience. **It is obedience**. The Bible tells us over and over to pursue joy.

Psalm 32:11
Be glad in the LORD, and rejoice, ye righteous: and shout for joy, all ye that are upright in heart.

Psalm 67:4a
O let the nations be glad and sing for joy...

Psalm 37:4a
Delight thyself also in the LORD....

Luke 10:20b
...but rather rejoice, because your names are written in heaven.

Philippians 4:4
Rejoice in the Lord always: and again I say, Rejoice.

Deuteronomy 28:47-48
Because you did not serve the Lord your God with joy and a glad heart...therefore you shall serve you enemies.

Psalm 16:11
...in Thy presence is fullness of joy.

We have God's Word which gives us an eternal perspective of the liberty we enjoy in Christ. God wants us to be proud of that liberty. He wants us to be grateful. He wants us to enjoy the benefits of Grace.

Living this good, joy filled life in Christ is a result of a deep and unwavering relationship with the Father. It is a joy that is grounded so firmly in a relationship with God that no assault of the devil or adverse circumstance could ever interrupt.

Galatians 5:22-23

But the fruit of the Spirit is love, joy, peace, longsuffering, gentleness, goodness, faith, meekness, temperance: against such there is no law. And they that are Christ's have crucified the flesh with the affections and lusts.

Fruit is the visible expression of power working inwardly. The invisible power of the Holy Spirit in those who are brought into living union with Christ produces a life regulated by the Holy Spirit; a life regulated by the character of God.

Romans 8:28

And we know that all things work together for good to them that love God, to them who are the called according to His purpose.

Romans 8:31b

...If God be for us, who can be against us?

Psalm 4:7

Thou hast put gladness in my heart...

Psalm 100:2

Serve the Lord with gladness; come before His presence with singing.

Philippians 4:4

Rejoice in the Lord always; and again I say, Rejoice.

Romans 5:1-6

Therefore being justified by faith, we have peace with God through our Lord Jesus Christ: By whom also we have access by faith into this grace wherein we stand, and rejoice in hope of the glory of God. And not only so, but we glory in tribulations also: knowing that tribulation worketh patience; And patience, experience; and experience, hope: And hope maketh not ashamed; because the love of God is shed abroad in our hearts by the Holy Ghost which is given unto us. For when we were yet without strength, in due time Christ died for the ungodly.

I Thessalonians 5:16

Rejoice evermore.

11. Rely on the Holy Spirit to keep the fire of passion burning (Jude 1:20).

Christianity is not something to be endured. It should be enjoyed. We should enjoy living a sinless life; enjoy our union with Christ. We are here to serve the Lord with gladness rather than out of obligation or duty.

Our liberty in Christ is much greater and so much grander than any temporary problem. Our temporary problems rob us of unrealized potential and unrealized living.

Problems are simply miracles not yet realized. If you want to see a miracle in your personal life, take your eyes off of you and your problems.

12. **Get involved in the ministry of the Lord Jesus Christ and refuse to quit.** Serving others makes life better for someone else. Give of your time, talents, and resources to a cause greater than yourself and watch God bring forth a miracle out of your problem. He majors in doing so.

All of us are have blood running warm in our veins, but not all of us are living. All of us will experience physical death, if Jesus tarries, but not all of us will enjoy eternal life.

Where the Presence of God is there is change. Where the Spirit of God is there is liberty; there is freedom.

Where the anointing is there is power; there is passion; there is boldness; there is change; there is deliverance; there is freedom. When the Spirit of Liberty is present, there is no fear; there is no bondage.

If there is no change, if there is no freedom, if there is no liberty, if there is no power, if there is no peace, **there is no God**. There may be religion, but not El-Elyon, the Most High God.

If there is bondage, there is no God. Where the Spirit of the Lord is there is emancipation from bondage. There is deliverance!!!

Let's consider these points as to why we should enjoy this Christian life.

1. God resides within. God is alive in us. We are partakers of God's divine nature.

II Corinthians 6:16

And what agreement hath the temple of God with idols? for ye are the temple of the living God; as God hath said, I will dwell in them, and walk in them; and I will be their God, and they shall be My people.

2. God has forgiven us and cleansed us of all sin past, present, and future.

I John 1:9

If we confess our sins, He is faithful and just to forgive us our sins, and to cleanse us from all unrighteousness.

3. God exchanged our filth for robes of righteousness.

Zechariah 3:4

And He answered and spake unto those that stood before Him, saying, Take away the filthy garments from him. And unto him He said, Behold, I have caused thine iniquity to pass from thee, and I will clothe thee with change of raiment.

4. God made Him who knew no sin to be made sin for us so that we might be made righteous.

II Corinthians 5:21
For He hath made Him to be sin for us, who knew no sin; that we might be made the righteousness of God in Him.

5. God adopted us as His children.

Ephesians 1:5
Having predestinated us unto the adoption of children by Jesus Christ to Himself, according to the good pleasure of His will,

6. God has put this treasure, the ministry of the Holy Spirit, in us.

I Corinthians 6:19
What? know ye not that your body is the temple of the Holy Ghost which is in you, which ye have of God, and ye are not your own?

7. God has sent us forth as His own ambassadors.

II Corinthians 5:20
Now then we are ambassadors for Christ, as though God did beseech you by us: we pray you in Christ's stead, be ye reconciled to God.

God wants us to demonstrate His power and love for His people through our obedience and through our liberty.

II Corinthians 3:16
Nevertheless when it shall turn to the Lord, the vail shall be taken away.

When we turn to Christ, God empowers us, through His Spirit within us, to be transfigured and live this abundant life. God did not save us to make life miserable for us. He came so that we might live!

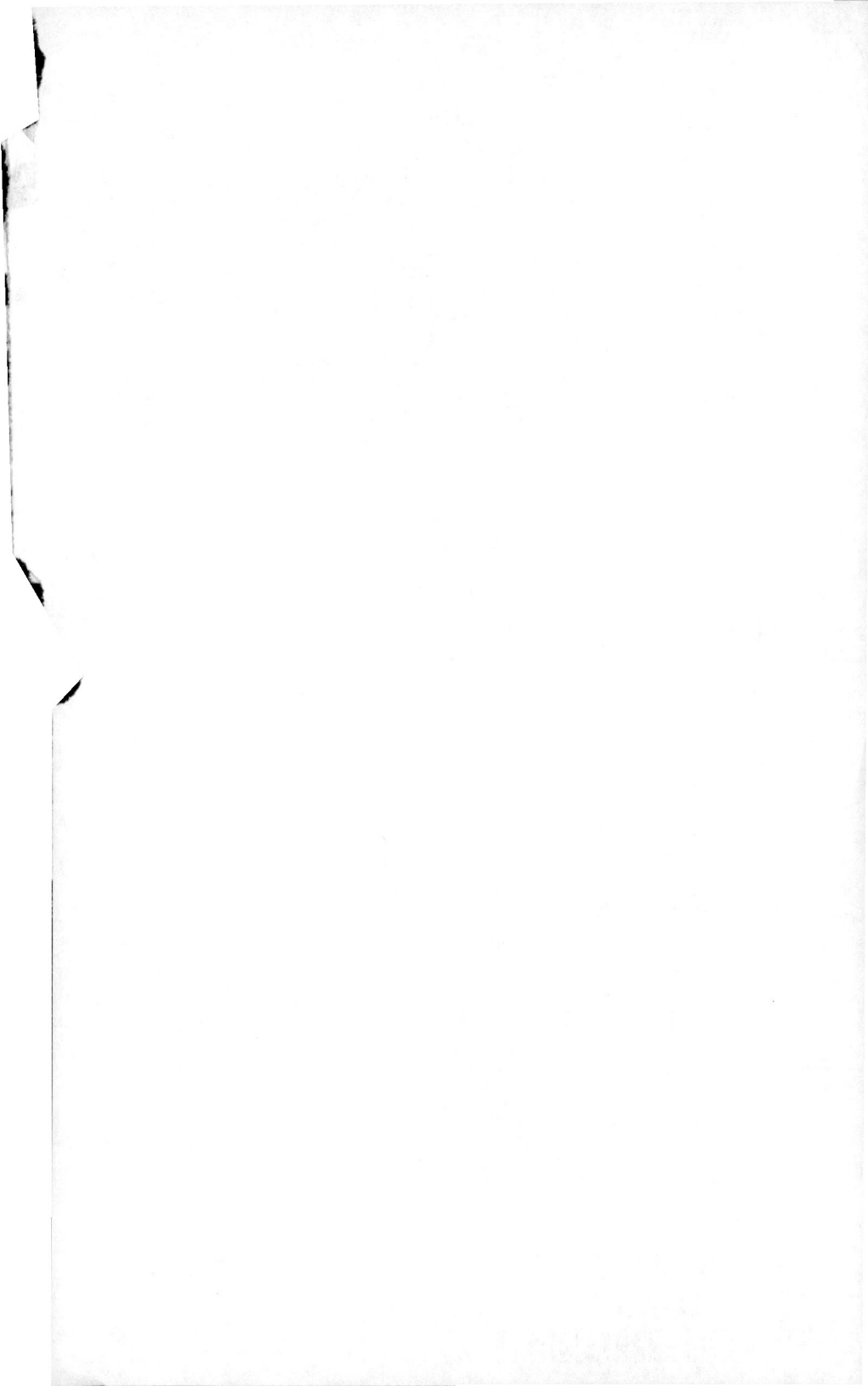

www.ingramcontent.com/pod-product-compliance
Lightning Source LLC
Chambersburg PA
CBHW021224020426
42331CB00003B/463